Unveiling Tweet Bots: Online Trust

Unveiling Tweet Bots: Online Trust

Marlon Shaun

Fate may twist, but our bond remains.

CONTENTS

CHAPTER 1

Book Introduction

1.1 Background

Social media bot detection has a decade of history. According to Cresci et al. [15], the first social media bot detector was made by Yardi et al. [60] who tried to detect spammers on Twitter. In the early days, most detection methods were based on supervised machine learning algorithms, and the detection was based solely on the information of individual accounts. However, as time went by, bots became more sophisticated and coordinated. Distinguishing bots from real accounts became almost impossible for humans [19]. At this point, due to the unavailability of ground truth data and due to the coordinated bot behaviour, researchers turned to other methods, namely, to unsupervised machine learning algorithms. These detectors, focused on groups of accounts rather than individual ones and aimed at detecting accounts with similar behavioural patterns. The problem with the earlier described methods is that detectors are only created once new previously undetectable bots are discovered, leaving significant life span for bots to operate. In order to solve this problem, researchers [17] today develop adversarial methods where they not only create detectors but also try to predict the evolution of bots to find vulnerabilities in their existing methods before they are exploited.

In order to combat malicious social media bots several institutions and universities have organized bot detection competitions. DARPA was a bot detection competition organized in 2015 [54] in order to test the effectiveness of influence bot detection methods. Recently the PAN 2019 Bots and Gender Profiling task has taken place, with the intention of using only the textual characteristics (Tweet) of social media accounts [46]. This has the advantage of creating platform-independent solutions as these methods do not rely on specific social media characteristics. The **book** work presented here will be based on the PAN 2019 Bots and Gender Profiling task and will aim at improving the results of the existing solutions which will be discussed in more detail in the literature review.

1.2   Motivation

Social media has changed how people acquire information and these platforms became an essential source of information for many [25]. Today, platforms such as Twitter have become a platform for manipulating public opinion and spreading or amplifying political misinformation. However, large scale manipulation and sharing of politically polarized content is not only done by humans but social media bots [8].

Bessi et al. [8] investigated the role of bots during the 2016 U.S. Presidential election. The researchers developed bot detection methods and estimated that about 400 000 bots were actively participating in political discussions generating roughly 3.8 million tweets which were about one-fifth of the entire conversation. Although at the time it was not clear, today we know that social media bots played a key role in the election [8] by spreading divisive messages which may have contributed to Trump's victory[1].

In their study, Stella et al. [50] analyzed the role of social bots during the Catalan Referendum of October 1, 2017, by observing the behaviour of the two opposite groups of polarities, the pro-independence and anti-independence. The study found that bots exploited and promoted content with the same polarity as the group they targeted. Furthermore, the group of pro-independence interacted with bots almost 100 times more than the opposite group of anti-independence, and in this group, bots had a larger influence and were spreading negative content and hatred in order to exacerbate online social conflict [50].

Bots almost always play a key role in political elections. During the Brexit referendum in the United Kingdom, they manipulated public opinion in favor of the country to leave the European Union [26]. Bots also interfered with the French presidential elections in 2017 by spreading the MacronLeaks campaign against Emmanuel Macron [22]. As we can see bots actively shape public opinion, usually by negative campaigning [26] and influence individuals who may not be able to distinguish between human or bot-generated content. Therefore, countermeasures have to be taken in order to neutralize bots that exploit and spread misinformation by creating state-of-the-art bot detection methods.

1.3   Problem Definition

The project will be based on the PAN 2019 Bots and Gender Profiling task [46] where author profiling had to be solved by classifying Twitter feeds as bots or humans, based solely on the account's textual form of the tweets without any additional information, such as tweet time, name, followers, accounts followed or profile picture. Furthermore, in the event where the feed belonged to a human, the gender of the user also had to be classified. The dataset consisted of 6760 labeled English and 4800 Spanish users, each with 100 tweets [1]. Additionally, bots were classified into the following subcategories which can help the model evaluation [2]:

1. Template: Bots which follow a predefined template.

2. Feed: Bots which retweet or share news about a certain topic.

3. Quote: Bots which tweet quotes from famous people.

4. Advanced: Bots which use advanced machine learning techniques to generate human like language.

This **book** work aims to research current state of the art approaches for bot detection and implement a deep-learning-based model that can predict whether a Twitter account belongs to a bot or a human based, solely on their tweets without additional information. The project will not implement the gender classification part of the PAN 2019 Bots and Gender Profiling task and will focus solely on the English dataset.

Furthermore, the **book** aims at answering the following research questions:

1. Can deep-learning-based approaches compete with classical machine learning methods on the limited dataset which was provided?

2. How would increasing the available data with data augmentation influence the performance of the models?

3. What is the effect of using pre-trained models and language representations on the results?

1.4 Equality and Ethics

Although Twitter and other social media platforms do not restrict the use of bots, they are often created to steal data or limit free speech [2, 8]. These actions break laws; therefore, they are also unethical. Having said that, bots can also be unethical and still be lawful, for example, by hiding their identity or spreading fake news [2]. In 2016, Microsoft launched its Twitter chatbot called Tay, which was developed to entertain people with casual conversations. Unfortunately, after hours of its launch, the friendly chatbot became racist due to malicious human interactions[2]. The question of who is responsible for the behaviour of automated accounts is challenging. Is it the developer's responsibility or is it the responsibility of those who teach it to behave in an unethical way? According to Alves et al. [2], this is determined whether the developer(s) knowingly designed their algorithms to behave maliciously or not; if so they will be responsible for its actions. However, if the developers followed industry guidelines and good development practices they cannot be held accountable.

Bot detectors also raise ethical questions. Social media platforms use different methods to determine the originality of accounts, and take actions against them. As most of these methods are based on machine learning algorithms, the results are accurate but not perfect; therefore, real human accounts can also be classified incorrectly as bots and may face restrictions to social media platforms [55]. To avoid incorrect classification, the algorithms and classification decision making have to be transparent. However, too much transparency may create more sophisticated bots [55], taking advantage of the transparency and spreading even more malicious information. Therefore, there is a trade off between accuracy and transparency and the correct balance has to be found during the development of detectors. Another ethical issue is the available resources and data which can be used for training detectors. For languages, such as English or Spanish, there are more data sets, more known bots and more resources to train unsupervised machine learning algorithms, whereas for other languages there are fewer. This means there could potentially be more undetected malicious automated accounts for languages that were not the primary focus of researchers.

1.5   Sustainability

Climate change is affecting every country, CO2 levels are at a record high[3] and electricity consumption is increasing year after year[4]. One of the goals of the United Nations is to combat global warming and to reduce carbon emissions[5]. Today, deep neural networks achieved impressive results in several Natural Language Processing (NLP) applications such as sentiment analysis, text classification or language translation mainly due to the available computational resources [53]. State-of-the-art machine learning algorithms are trained on specialized hardware such as GPUs or TPUs, sometimes for weeks or months, which require high electricity consumption. Even though clean energy is becoming more common, non-renewable energy still counts as the main source of energy[6]. This has a substantial cost to the environment. Strubbel et al. [53] analyzed the cost and energy consumption of several NLP models. The results show the computational costs are between \$41-\$3000000 and the CO2 emissions range from 27lbs to 626155lbs, where the lower end models are transformer models, whereas the upper end models are neural architecture search (NAS) models. In comparison, the carbon foot print of one passenger for a flight from New York to San Francisco is less than 2000lbs [53]. This comparison shows just how important it is to write efficient code and how important it is to develop methods that speed up the training phase.

Although the bot detectors which will be introduced later in the **book** fall on the lower end of the spectrum of energy consumption, training the models on servers using Intel Xeon CPUs or Nvidia Tesla P100-PCIE-16GB GPUs took around three and a half hours. With that being said, hundreds of computational hours have been spent on training and developing the bot detector, which according, to my estimations, has a carbon footprint of around 10lbs.

1.6 Book Structure

The **book** structure is organized as follows:

- Chapter 2: Relevant research on Twitter, bots and different bot detection methods are reviewed. In addition, the chapter also focuses on how datasets can be collected, what bot detection challenges researchers faced and the top 3 best performing solutions of the the PAN 2019 Bots and Gender Profiling task are discussed.

- Chapter 3: Introduces the reader to the theoretical background, algorithms and methods of deep-learning-based bot detectors.

- Chapter 4: Describes the architecture and design of the bot detectors created in this work.

- Chapter 5: Evaluates the proposed models on the test set.

- Chapter 6: Discusses the results of the models.

- Chapter 7: Summarizes the most important findings of the **book** and discusses future improvements.

CHAPTER 2

Literature Review

2.1 Twitter

Twitter is a popular social media networking service in San Fransisco, California, established by Jack Dorsey, Noah Glass, Biz Stone, and Evan Williams in 2006. Twitter is a microblogging service, which means that the information shared, i.e the tweets (small messages), are limited to a small size of 280 characters, making them easy to read and write [41]. Tweets are similar to emails or blogs; they allow users to share their experiences and ideas with any member on the platform. Users can post, like, retweet, follow other users; furthermore each user has their own timeline where their posts are collected. When users retweet, they forward a tweet to their own followers [37] and although one can retweet in order to disagree with an opinion[1] as Metaxas et al. [37], show a retweet usually indicates agreement, trust and interest in a message. When someone starts following a user, such as a friend, a company or a celebrity, they get a stream of the following users' tweets [41]. Moreover, users can mention and reply to others using the sign "@" followed by the target username, which creates a two-way communication channel. Users can also group posted tweets by a topic using hashtags, which are words prefixed by the hash symbol "#".

As of Q1 2019, Twitter was estimated to have 330 million monthly active users[2], and 187 million daily active users[3]. This is a substantial growth compared to its 30 million monthly active users in Q1[3] 2010 and making it one of the most visited websites with around 6 billion daily visits[4]. Furthermore, today more than a billion Tweets are created each week[5].

As of today, Twitter is not only a social media platform where individuals can share their opinions, but it has also become one of the key real time communication channels during natural disasters and political events [41]. In addition, Twitter became one of the most important platforms where politicians can communicate their campaign messages, mobilize their supporters and influence the public agenda [52]. For example, on the 2016 presidential Election Day, more than 75 million tweets were posted, which is far more than the 31 million during the 2012 elections[6].

The authors of Uddin et al. [56] conducted a study in which 716 randomly selected Twitter profiles were used to identify six classes of Twitter users:

1. Personal users: Users who use the platform for fun, learn or read news, do not promote any business or product, and their social interactions are considered to be low or mild.

2. Professional users: Home users who have many followers and follow many. They mainly focus on one area by sharing useful information about it.

3. Business users: Users who frequently tweet but have little interactions. Their behavior follows a similar pattern to each other, following a marketing and business strategy.

4. Spam users: Randomly follow users and spread malicious tweets, their behavior follows the same pattern to each other.

5. Feed/News: These accounts post news-related tweets. They are not interactive.

6. Viral/Marketing Services: Accounts that serve to increase sales, brand awareness or marketing objectives.

The first three of the above-mentioned user classes belong to human accounts, whereas the last three to machines also known as digital actors or bots. In the next section digital actors, or bots, will be discussed in more detail.

2.2 Bots

Bots, agents or actors, are applications that can execute predefined tasks and do so repetitively. Moreover, social media bots or spambots are a special type of bots which act as humans hidden behind social media accounts interacting with humans and influencing them with political, ideological, or commercial purposes [59]. In 2016, nearly 19% of all tweets related to the US election were generated by bots, and these tweets were retweeted almost at the same rate as if they had been originated by human accounts [8]. Today, bots are able to create human-like tweets and form botnets spreading malicious information even faster.

In their paper, Stieglitz et al. [51] ask how social media bots can be distinguished from one another. Ferrara et al. [23] distinguish two types of bots, namely, benign bots and harmful bots. Benign bots aggregate content, automatically respond to inquiries, and in general, can be useful. On the other hand harmful or malicious bots are designed for harmful purposes [51]. As Ferrara et al. [23] highlight, benign bots can also be harmful, for example by spreading unverified information. Boshmaf et al. [9] distinguish social bots and other bots based on whether a bot is trying to hide its identity. Social media bots act and pretend to be real social media users by simulating human behavior and manipulating public opinion using artificial intelligence [9].

There is an intermediate class of bots called hybrid social bots (cyborgs) where once a human registers an account the user can automate specific tasks such as posting automatic tweets. In this case, hybrid social bots are either human-assisted bots or bot-assisted humans [14], where humans are responsible for content production and creation [1]. Moreover, hybrid bots are an effective and low-cost approach to gain influence on social media [1]. Bots can also form together and create botnets or armies where bots coordinate and follow each other [57]. Boshmaf et al. [9] define a Socialbot Network (SbN) as "a set of socialbots that are owned and maintained by a human controller called the botherder". These networks have three components [9]:

1. Socialbots: Control a social media account and can execute commands sent by the botmaster such as to post a message or interact with other users.

2. Botmaster: A social media-independent software which the botherder uses to define commands to be executed by the bots.

3. Command & Control channel: A communication channel between the social bots and the botmaster.

While early bots were naïve and easy to spot, on platforms such as Twitter, bots today became increasingly sophisticated, making their detection very difficult [51]. Many of these bots create their own profiles by stealing users' identities, making conversations using Natural Language Processing (NLP) and aiming to strengthen their influence by increasing the number of their followers [51].

2.3 Twitter Bots

A bot on Twitter is a special type of account controlled by a machine rather than a human. These accounts can automatically tweet, re-tweet, like, follow/unfollow and send direct messages. Twitter does not restrict the use of bots as long as they follow the automation rules[7]. Bots can broadcast helpful information, respond to users in direct messages or try new solutions which help people[8]. On the other hand, bots are not supposed to spam, spread misinformation or violate any other policies [8].

However, Twitter bots are similar to regular bots, they can be benign, broadcasting news and helpful information, but they can also be harmful, spreading misinformation and promoting hate speech. There are different types of Twitter bots. The purpose of fake follower bots is to increase the number of followers of a target account [16]. While they may seem harmless, artificially increasing someone's followers by fake accounts makes them more influential and seem more trustworthy than they are, and as a result, people are more likely to follow them [16].

A study conducted by Varol et al. [57] shows that around 15% of Twitter accounts are bots. While this is a very high number, as demonstrated by Varol et al., this may still be an underestimation as increasing evidence suggests the presence of hybrid human-bot accounts, which need some human supervision [57]; therefore, the actual number of automated accounts could be higher.

2.4 Bot Detection Methods

This section discusses the different types of methods, their features, evaluation metrics and datasets used for detecting bots. Moreover, the evolution of bot detectors and bots will also be discussed in this chapter.

2.4.1 Evolution of Social Media Bots and Their Detectors

Cresci et al. [15] distinguish three major waves of different characteristics of bots. During the first wave, until around 2011, Online Social Networks (OSNs) had simplistic bots, which showed clear signs of automation with little social interactivity and their purpose was solely spam related. On the other hand, the second wave of social bots increased their social interactivity by following each other (creating bot nets) and had detailed profiles. Moreover, these bots were more sophisticated, not spamming the same messages over and over again. Lastly the third wave of bots mimic human behavior, have a large number of real followers as well as friends and typically share malicious messages with many neutral ones [15].

As bots were evolving, so were their detectors. According to Cresci et al. [15], the first social network bot detection method dates back to 2010, when detectors were based on supervised machine learning algorithms where the classification was based solely on the information of the account which was being detected. These detectors operated on the assumption that bots had individual characteristics which could be used to distinguish them from human accounts. As bots became more sophisticated with the third wave of bots, detecting them with supervised methods assuming that bots are separable from real human accounts was no longer possible [15]. Rather than classifying accounts one by one, researchers targeted groups of accounts [15, 11], as these bots coordinate with one another and leave traces of synchronization behind [15]. Many of these bot detectors are unsupervised or semi-supervised in order to generalize the flaws of supervised methods which are limited by data availability [15].

When new types of bots that cannot be detected by available solutions are discovered, researchers start developing detection systems capable of detecting them. As Cresci et al. [15] describe, this results in a lag between the development of detectors and the deployment of them; thus bots have a large time span when they can operate. Moreover, "scholars and OSN administrators are constantly one step behind of malicious account developers"; therefore, the influence of bots do not seem to decrease on social media networks [15]. In order to mitigate these challenges in the future, adversarial machine learning techniques could be used [15]. As most machine learning models are incorrectly based on the assumption that the test data is drawn from the same distribution as the train data, the accuracy of the models can degrade in the case of adversaries [24]. Adversarial machine learning is a machine learning paradigm based on creating data that is first based on legitimate data, but through perturbation, the model is being fooled and incorrectly classifies the sample; thus, model vulnerabilities can be detected before they are exploited by adversaries [24].

2.4.2 Data Collection

While the performance of the models does depend on the model configurations, the datasets used for training the models are just as or even more important than the models themselves. In their study, Beskow et al. [7] demonstrate four tiers of Twitter data based on data availability which can be used for training machine learning models. As the study shows there is a tradeoff between data richness and computational time to classify accounts. While a Tier 1 model is suitable for classifying accounts in a large data stream where the account metadata with a tweet is available, Tier 3 is suitable for problems where high accuracy is expected, using all available information of an account [7]. As table 2.1 demonstrates, using a Tier 0 dataset, the classification is instant, whereas a model trained on a Tier 3 dataset takes around 20 hours.

Annotating Twitter accounts as bots or humans is a challenging task. In their study, Cresci et al. [19] performed a crowdsourcing campaign where 247 real-world trusted twitter users from 42 different countries were asked to classify an already labeled set of Twitter accounts. The dataset consisted of 4428 accounts of humans and bots, where each account had to be classified by at least 3 contributors; thus, the class was decided by majority voting [19]. The results show that the accuracy by human classification was less than 24% for social bots, classifying more than 1000 social bots as humans (False

Negative). Human and traditional bot accounts had been classified correctly with 91% and 92% accuracy. The study shows that humans may not be able to detect social bots and distinguish them from real human accounts [19]. Therefore, manually creating ground-truth datasets is not applicable for sophisticated social bots, so Cresci et al. [19] suggest the use of a new annotation method which takes into account the similarities and the behavior of the accounts.

In their study Almaatouq et al. [1] created a dataset based on the accounts which had been suspended by Twitter. The authors collected tweets and user information during a period of one month, using the Twitter public streaming API and labeled the accounts as spammers which were later suspended or removed. As a result, 7% of the dataset were classified as bots. As the authors highlight, the classified accounts may contain accounts which had been deactivated by the users themselves, but the vast majority, 93% of the suspensions, are a result of spamming behavior [1].

In their study, Lee et al. [31] deployed 60 honeypot accounts on Twitter which were designed to avoid interacting with regular users and could tweet normal text, mention other honeypot accounts, tweet a link or tweet one of Twitters top 10 topics. These honeypot accounts reported which accounts interacted with them, such as started following them. As the honeypots posted random messages and only interacted with other honeypots, a human would not find them interesting. Therefore, accounts which started following them or interacted with them should not be legitimate accounts. The study conducted by Lee et al. [31] concluded that Twitter suspended around 23% of the accounts which had been reported by the honeypots. Although 77% of the reported accounts were not suspended by Twitter, the researchers clustered the accounts and came to the conclusion that they were content polluters.

Other ways to collect data is by labeling accounts that participated in known bot attacks. Beskhow et al. [7] collected bot accounts during a Twitter bot attack against NATO and

Tier	Description	Focus	Collect/process Time per 250 Accounts	# of Data Entities (i.e tweets)
Tier 0	Tweet text only	Semantics	N/A**	1
Tier 1	Account + 1 Tweet	Account Meta-data	1.9 seconds	2
Tier 2	Account + Time-line	Temporal patterns	3.7 minutes	200+
Tier 3	Account + Time-line + Friends Timeline	Network patterns	20 hours	50,000+

Table 2.1: Four tiers of Twitter data. Source: [7]

the DFR Lab in 2017. On average, these accounts have 130 and 43 interactions on a daily basis [7]. On the other hand, during the attack, they averaged 6000 interactions per hour. The authors [7] were able to label 99% of this activity as bot activity; by manually verifying them using random sampling. Moreover, 8 months later, Twitter had suspended 95.5% of the accounts [7].

Many studies used a variety of the above-mentioned data collection methods. Varol et al. [57] trained their models using manually labeled accounts, both manual and honeypot collected accounts and a mixture of these two with different ratios. Cresci et al. [16] created a bot dataset by buying 3000 fake accounts from different Twitter online markets and Chu et al. [14] manually analyzed the accounts which they have collected using the Twitter API using a Depth-First Search (DFS) approach.

2.4.3 Modeling Approaches

This section discusses the different types of modeling approaches used in the cited papers. The section is divided into five subsections which go into depth about rule-based, supervised, unsupervised and adversarial methods. Finally, these methods are discussed and compared with one another.

Rule-Based Methods

Cresci et al. [16] used the Camisani-Calzolari rule set (CC) [10], which assigns an account positive human/active and negative bot/inactive scores. Based on the two scores, the classification of an account can be given by calculating the distance between the two scores. If the sum of the scores is greater than 0, the account is considered human; if it is between 0 and -4, it is neutral; otherwise the account is classified as a bot. The algorithm uses a set of human criterion, such as whether the profile contains an image, physical address or if at least one of its tweets has been re-twitted by other accounts and if so, one human point is given. On the other hand, one bot point is given for each human criterion that cannot be verified and two bot points if the account only uses APIs. Other rule-based methods include the Socialbakers rule set, which determines the classification based on 8 rules, such as whether the account has ever tweeted, the percentage of links in tweets or if the account uses spam phrases in its tweets [16].

Supervised Methods

Machine learning algorithms can be characterized based on the desired outcome of the algorithm [43]. Supervised methods generate a function that maps the inputs into desired outputs based on the input-output pairs on which the model is trained. Therefore, human and bot related labeled data can be fed to a machine learning algorithm that can be trained to classifying unforeseen accounts [30].

Most papers reviewed and cited in this literature review utilize supervised machine learning methods in order to detect social media bots. Moreover, Cresci et al. [15] reviewed 236 bot detectors published since 2010, and the majority of the detectors are based on supervised algorithms. Most papers use classical machine learning methods [59, 45, 30, 56, 16, 57, 7, 31, 1, 14] such as Random Forest (RF), Logistic Regression (LR), AdaBoost (AB), Decision Tree (DT), Support Vector Machine (SVM) or Naïve Bayes (NB). However, deep-learning-based approaches are also researched [30].

Below, I discuss three papers in more detail, two of which use classical machine learning methods and one using deep learning. These papers are examined here as they represent different types of approaches and for many authors they have served as benchmarks and reference studies.

BotoMeter was developed at Indiana University and has been a publicly available service since 2014 to determine whether an English Twitter account is human or machine. The system can be accessed via REST call APIs or via a website. BotoMeter calculates a score called the bot-likelihood score of a given account and returns it to the user. The classification consists of several steps. First, more than 1000 features are extracted from a given account, such as network features (retweets or mentions), user features (user location, account creation date or language), features regarding friends, temporal features (tweet rate), content features and sentiment features. Next, a random forest classifier predicts whether the account is a machine or a human. The model has been trained on 31k accounts (15k accounts belonging to bots, 16k to humans) and 5.6 million tweets based on the dataset collected by Lee et al. [59]. The model achieved a 0.95 AUC, and every day more than a quarter-million requests are served [59].

Pozzana et al. [45] in their study used two datasets, one dataset which the researchers labeled with BotoMeter of the French Elections and another created by Cresci et al., which contains social spambots. The dataset was organized into sessions, which are the consecutive tweets posted by the same user and separated from the previous tweet by T minutes. The researchers extracted features, such as the fraction of retweets, fraction of replies, the number of mentions in a tweet or the length of the tweet itself. Four supervised machine learning algorithms were trained using 10-fold cross-validation with different combinations of features, namely Decision Tree (DT), Extra Trees (ET), Random Forest (RF) and AdaBoost (AB). All models reported an Area Under the Receiver Operating Characteristic Curve (ROC AUC) of 97% except for the AB, which scored 84%.

Kudugunta et al. [30] aimed at solving account-level and tweet-level bot detection, using deep learning and classical machine learning methods. For the account level classification, the researchers used user metadata to determine the classification, and AUC of 98.45% was achieved with RF. However, the researchers managed to increase the accuracy of account-level classification to 98.81% using AdaBoost and by balancing the dataset via oversampling techniques, namely Synthetic Minority Oversampling Technique (SMOTE)

[12]. Regarding the tweet-level detection, the researcher first preprocessed the tweets by tokenizing them, replacing hashtags, URLs, numbers, emojis and mentions with tags and converting all letters to lowercase. Then the tokenized tweets were transformed into embeddings using Global Vectors for Word Representation (GloVE), and the sequence was fed into Long Short Term Memory models. Moreover, the researchers also created Contextual LSTM models (which are a special type of LSTM models with multiple inputs and outputs), which were trained on the tweet's embedding along with user metadata. The LSTM model trained on tweets only, reached 95% accuracy, whereas the best contextual LSTM network achieved about 96%.

Unsupervised Methods

Due to the drawback of supervised machine learning approaches, such as the limited availability of ground-truth and reliable training datasets [36], researchers during the past years have shifted to unsupervised methods [15]. While supervised machine learning algorithms learn on labeled data, unsupervised methods learn patterns from untagged data, such as by clustering accounts. Moreover, most of the unsupervised approaches are group-based; that is, the analysis is based on groups of accounts rather than individual accounts; therefore, they are effective at identifying coordinated and synchronized accounts [15]. Although most approaches use connectivity patterns, such as directed graphs in order to identify bots with similar behavior [15, 28], other approaches identify bots by spotting anomalous tweeting and retweeting patterns [15, 11, 28].

An example of an unsupervised approach is DeBot [11], a social media bot detection method that correlates millions of users in near real-time to identify bot accounts. DeBot is based on a lag-sensitive hashing technique, which hashes the correlated users into the same buckets based on the users wrapping correlation. The system developed by Chavoshi et al. [11] calculates the correlation of the users based on user actions, such as posting, sharing, liking tweeting, retweeting or deleting. This sequence, including a time stamp, forms a time series; thus, the method aims to identify accounts with similar activity patterns. The architecture of DeBot consists of four components:

1. Collector: Collects tweets for a given set of keywords for T hours and creates the time series of the users with one second sampling time.

2. Indexer: Hashes each time series into buckets and reports suspicious users in a given bucket.

3. Listener: Collects and creates the activity time series of the suspicious users employing all user activities.

4. Validator: Calculates a wrapped correlation matrix of the suspicious users and clusters them. Users belonging to a cluster are reported as bots.

DeBot has been compared against Twitter's suspension process by identifying accounts as bots over a given period of time and every few days checking if the identified accounts has been suspended by Twitter. After 12 weeks, 45% of the accounts identified as bots by DeBot were also been suspended by Twitter. In addition, DeBot identifies bots at a higher rate than Twitter, which could mean Twitter does not suspend each identified bot.

Mazza et al. [36] created an unsupervised group based bot detection method called Retweet-Buster (RTBust). RTBust consists of 3 logical components. First, during the data preparation phase, retweet time series are created and compressed using Run-length Encoding (RLE) to minimize the amount of data to process and maximize the information of the time series. Next, a dimensionality reduction technique is used, namely Variational Autoencoders (VAEs), which learns the latent features of the data by using an LSTM based encoder and decoder. Finally, Hierarchical-based Clustering (HDBSCAN) is used to cluster the users. Large clusters may indicate synchronized accounts. Therefore, they are labeled as bots, where as human accounts are considered as noise. The authors experimented with different configurations and different dimensionality reduction methods, such as Principal Component Analysis (PCA) and Time Independent Component Analysis (TICA). The results show that the best model using VAE achieved an F1 score of 0.87.

Adversarial Methods

All bot detection methods mentioned so far has been created following a reactive schema where suspicious OSN behaviors are first detected and then studied, and finally, new detection methods are designed and deployed [17]. Therefore, as described by Cresci et al. [17], scholars and OSN administrators are always one step behind of bot developers. A proactive approach on the other hand would consist of two models. First, a simulation model would produce representations of malicious accounts that do not exist yet, but are similar to existing ones. Then, each representation would be evaluated, and those that are able to evade detection are considered threat and need to be taken into consideration during the development and design of new detectors [17]. This approach could have the advantage of foreseeing future bot evolutions and taking countermeasures before the actual evolution takes place. Figure 2.1 demonstrates the two different types of schemes described above.

Following the proactive scheme (Figure 2.1) Cresci et al. [17] have created a simulation model using a Genetic Algorithm (GA) based on digital DNA modeling. The Digital modeling technique creates a string representation of the user's online actions, where each action, such as a tweet, is represented as a character, such as a "T", and these actions encoded as characters form the digital DNA. Then the genetic algorithm using mutation and crossover generates new sequences of digital DNA of bots, which are evaluated against a bot detector. The authors have used DNA fingerprinting to detect bots which, given a list of digital DNAs, compares them and finds similarities of automated accounts by calculating the Longest Common Substring (LCS) of their DNA. Accounts sharing a long LCS or behavior pattern are likely to be similar as well. Moreover, Cresci et al. [17] show

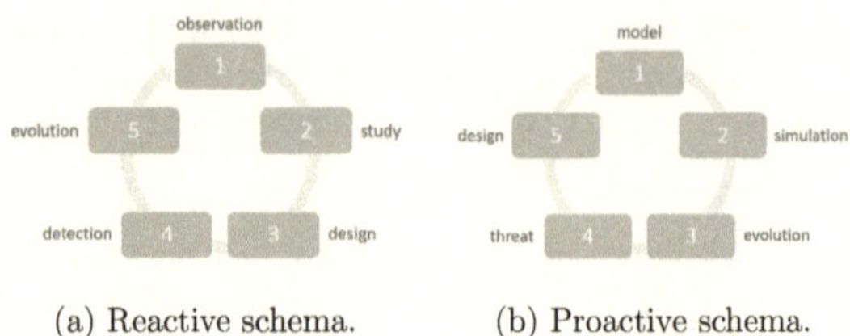

(a) Reactive schema.   (b) Proactive schema.

Figure 2.1: Source: From reaction to proaction: Unexplored ways to the detection of evolving spambots [17]

that bots have long LCS even with large numbers of accounts, whereas human accounts show little similarity. The authors have designed and launched multiple experiments and demonstrated that using the above-mentioned methods, newly evolved bots can avoid detection.

Discussion

Table 2.2 shows information of the inspected papers such as the type of approach the authors used and algorithms. Table 2.3 shows the results of the papers. As we can see, most researchers used supervised machine learning algorithms. Moreover, classical machine learning algorithms were the most common. Authors of [59, 45, 18] used unsupervised methods, whereas the author of [16] created detectors using a rule-based approach, while the rest of the authors created supervised bot detectors. It is important to highlight that the models had been trained and evaluated on different datasets, with different features and evaluation metrics; therefore, they cannot be directly compared to one another.

Researcher(s)	Type	Algorithm(s)
Cresci et al. [16]	Rule Based	CC
Yang et al.[59]	Supervised	RF
Pozzana et al. [45]	Supervised	RF, DT, ET, AB
Mazza et al. [36]	Unsupervised	RTBust (VAE)
Chavoshi et al. [11]	Unsupervised	DeBot
Varol et al. [57]	Supervised	RF, AB, LR, DT
Beskow et al. [7]	Supervised	NB, LR, SVM, DT, RF
Lee et al. [31]	Supervised	30 classifiers, best RF
Almaatouq et al. [1]	Supervised	ZeroR, BN, NB, LR, DT, RF
Chu et al. [14]	Supervised	RF
Kudugunta et al [30]	Supervised	LR, AB, LSTM
Cresci et al. [18]	Unsupervised	GA

Table 2.2: Summary of the cited papers.

Researcher(s)	Algorithm	Acc.	Prec.	Recall	F_1	MCC	AUC
Cresci et al. [16]	CC	0.55	0.98	0.06	0.12	0.18	
Yang et al.[59]	RF						0.95
Pozzana et al. [45]	RF						0.97
	DT						0.97
	ET						0.97
	AB						0.84
Mazza et al. [36]	RTBust (VAE)	0.87	0.93	0.81	0.87	0.76	
Chavoshi et al. [11]	DeBot		0.94				
Varol et al. [57]	RF						0.95
Beskow et al. [7]	NB	0.61	0.56	0.99			0.89
	LR	0.67	1.0	0.32			0.92
	SVM	0.90	0.85	0.97			0.95
	DT	0.96	0.96	0.97			0.96
	RF	0.98	0.99	0.97			0.99
Lee et al. [31]	RF	0.98				0.98	0.99
Chu et al. [14]	RF	0.96					

Table 2.3: Results of the papers

2.5 Overview of the Best Results of the Author Profiling Task

This section summarizes the top 3 highest performing approaches of the 7th International Author Profiling Shared Task at PAN 2019, focusing solely on the English bot detection challenge. Moreover, the results highlighted here will serve as a benchmark for the bot detection model proposed in the methodology chapter of the **book**.

Johanson et al. [29] have achieved the highest accuracy of the bot detection challenge [46]. As a first step, the authors extracted several tweet level features, such as tweet length, number of capital letters/URLs/mentions etc., and created account-based statistics of these features. The similarity of subsequent tweets of different accounts was also calculated, using the Damerau-Levenshtein distance, and the most common unigrams and bigrams were extracted by applying tf-idf to the concatenated tweets belonging to the same account. The authors used two classifiers; first, a logistic regression classifier was trained on the tf-idf features, and then the output of the LR along with the statistical features was fed to a random forest classifier. The authors achieved an accuracy of 0.95, the best result for the bot detection task.

Meanwhile, Fernquist [21] extracted three main features. First, features from tf-idf were extracted from the concatenated tweets of an account, just as in [29]. Then compression features were extracted by compressing the concatenated tweets of each user and extracting statistical features from them. And lastly, tweet features were extracted, such as the retweet ratio, Shannon entropy of all tweets concatenated or the number of hashtags used divided by the total number of hashtags. The researchers trained a CatBoost classifier with 4158 features and reached an accuracy of 0.949.

Bacciu et al. [3] extracted tweet level features such as the average number of emojis used in each tweet, links shared or the average number of hashtags used. Furthermore, cosine similarity was calculated, sentiment analysis was applied to each tweet and text distortion was used to emphasize the use of special characters. The classifier consists of two layers. The first layer consists of an SVM and an AdaBoost instance, whereas the second layer has a Soft-Voting classifier that ensemble the predictions of the first layer. The classifier described reached an accuracy of 0.94, making it the third-best performing classifier.

As can be seen, the best performing approaches all reached more than 0.94 accuracy. In addition they all used classical machine learning algorithms. The organizers of the PAN 2019 challenge [46] have evaluated all 46 submitted approaches, and the majority of them used classical machine learning approaches with only a few using deep learning methods.

CHAPTER 3

Theory

3.1 Introduction

This section introduces the fundamentals of natural language processing and the algorithms of the proposed bot detection models. Moreover, this section aims to explain design choices of the implementation phase, such as why certain algorithms are used instead of others. Furthermore, this section will also discuss the challenges that need to be overcome and the methods available to increase the accuracy of bot detectors.

As seen in the literature review, bot detection methods are usually based on supervised or unsupervised approaches sometimes combined with adversarial methods. Since this work is based on the PAN 2019 Bots and Gender Profiling task where labeled tweets were the only source of data, the work presented in this book work is based on supervised machine learning methods where the prediction whether an account is a human or a bot is based on the inspected account's tweets without additional information. Therefore, the task which is being solved is considered a text classification problem. In addition, as most submissions of the PAN 2019 Bots and Gender Profiling task are based on classical machine learning algorithms (see the literature review for more details) which are already well explored, or those based on deep learning methods did not achieve high accuracy, the proposed bot detectors in chapter 4 will be based solely on deep learning methods. Thus this chapter will also only focus on this research area.

3.2 Fundamentals of the proposed bot detector

This section describes the most important algorithms and methods that the proposed bot detectors build on.

3.2.1 Artificial neural networks

Artificial Neural Networks (ANNs) are computational units inspired by biological neurons, first researched during the 1940s [27]. ANNs are well suited for a variety of tasks, including classification problems. The simplest form of an ANN consists of one artificial neuron, also called a perceptron. A perceptron consists of n inputs $x_i \in X$, weights $w_i \in \mathbb{R}$ and a bias $b \in \mathbb{R}$ where w_i corresponds to the weight of x_i and determines the importance of the input (see figure 3.1). The neuron's output is calculated by adding the weighed sum of the inputs to the bias and applying the result to an activation function σ (see equation 3.1 [40]). The activation function determines how the inputs are transformed into outputs. There are several activation functions such as the sigmoid, relu or the step function [40].

$$Y = \sigma \left(\sum_{i=1}^{n} x_i w_i + b \right) \tag{3.1}$$

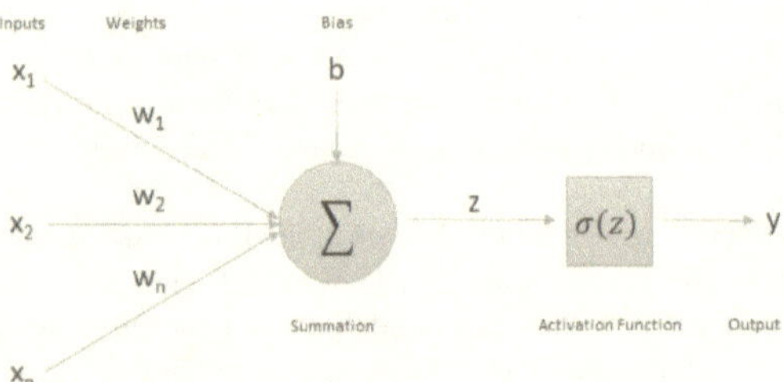

Figure 3.1: Architecture of a perceptron.

ANNs can consist of a single layer of neurons or multiple layers. Single-layer networks organize neurons into a single layer, whereas multi-layer networks have multiple layers of neurons and usually consist of an input layer, hidden layer and output layer. They are also called multilayer perceptrons (MLPs) (see figure 3.2).

ANNs learn by tuning their parameters using backpropagation algorithms. During the training phase, each training sample is fed into the network and an error value is calculated based on a cost function. The backpropagation algorithm sends back the error to the network, calculates the gradient of the loss function and updates the weights in order to reduce the error.

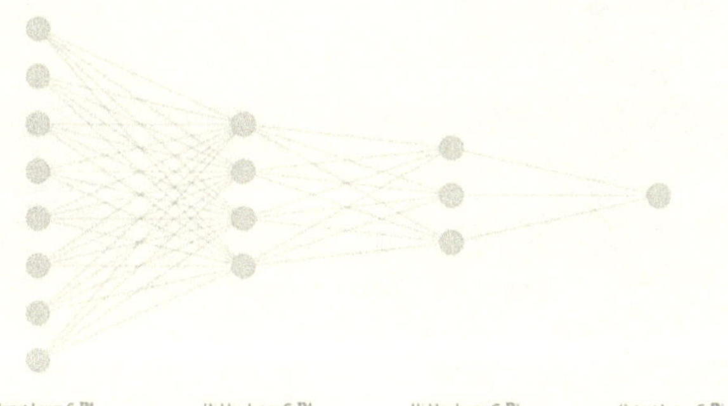

Figure 3.2: MLP with one input layer, two hidden layers and one output layer.

3.2.2 Recurrent neural networks

The problems with ANNs in regard to NLP applications is that they cannot handle and learn long dependencies. Moreover, ANNs need to use fixed lengths context which needs to be specified during the design phase of the model [38]. On the other hand, Recurrent neural networks (RNNs) use recurrent connections to allow information to cycle within the network and for information to persist [38, 42] while processing variable length inputs. This allows RNNs to learn correlations between data points that are close in the sequence [48].

Figure 3.3 shows the basic architecture of RNNs as well as unfolded in time. Instead of using a fixed number of inputs, RNNs are fed one input x_i at a time and the network predicts h_i for each input. As can be seen, the loop passes the information from one step to the next allowing the network to learn from previous states.

In order to use future information, Schuster et al. [48] proposed an RNN architecture consisting of two RNN networks. The two networks can be combined where each network learns from the input data for both time directions (forward/backward). These RNN networks are called bi-directional RNNs (BRNNs).

Unfortunately RNNs are unable to learn long dependencies due to the gradient vanishing and exploding problems [4]. In order to solve this issue researchers have developed novel approaches such as Long Short Term Memory (LSTM) networks or Gated Recurrent Unit networks (GRUs) which overcome the drawbacks of traditional RNNs.

3.2.3 LSTM

The key idea behind LSTMs is that at each time step the network passes a cell state and a hidden state to the next step. The cell state contains information for the entire

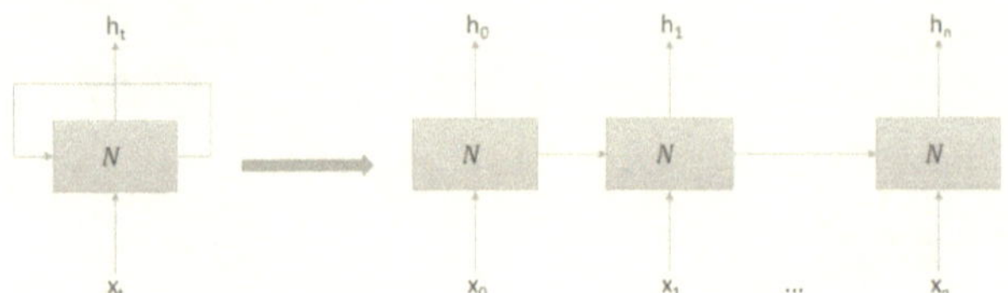

Figure 3.3: Architecture of ANNs

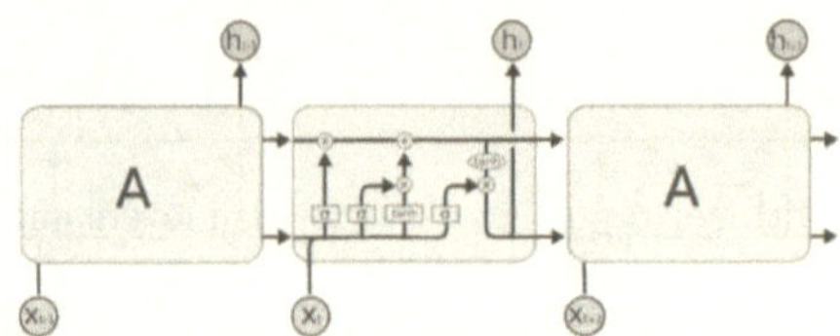

Figure 3.4: LSTM Architecture: [42]

sequence and can be considered as a long term memory. On the other hand, the hidden state contains information about the previous state. LSTMs consist of multiple gates which control the flow of information [42] (see Figure 3.4). LSTMs have three gates composed of a sigmoid neural net layer and a pointwise multiplication operation. The sigmoid layer determines how much information should be passed through. Folowing are the three gates:

1. Forget gate: Decides the information to keep from the previous hidden state and concatenates the current input to it.

2. Input gate: Decides what information to store in the cell state based on the concatenated previous hidden state and the current input.

3. Output gate: Computes the new hidden state based on the newly calculated cell state, the concatenated previous hidden state and current inputs.

3.2.4   Data augmentation

Data augmentation has shown promising results in computer vision, even by using simple techniques such as cropping, rotating and flipping images which became a great way to reduce overfitting of models [44]. However, augmenting textual data is a challenging task as there are neither generalized rules nor best practices for transforming this type of data. Yu et al.[61] generated new data by translating sentences from English to French and back to English. Other approaches include replacing words by their synonyms or using data noising as smoothing [58]. Wei et al. [58] developed a data augmentation technique to improve the performance of text classification models. The technique consists of synonym replacement, random insertion, random swap and random deletion. The results show an average of around 1% absolute increase in performance but on small datasets the method boosted the performance by even 3%.

3.2.5 Hyper-parameter optimization

Typically ANN-based models have between 10 to 50 hyper-parameters to be configured before training the model [6]. This is a difficult task and it is often considered an art rather than science since [6] there is no rule on how machine learning models should be configured as the parameters may change from one problem to another. Hyper-parameter optimization aims to answer the question of how optimal hyper-parameters can be chosen for a given machine learning algorithm. The most popular approaches that will be discussed here include grid search, Bayesian optimization and random search.

Grid Search: It is one of the most widely used automatic strategies for hyper parameter optimization [5]. During the parameter tuning, a subset of the hyper-parameter space has to be manually specified. The algorithm trains the model on each pair of the specified parameters, evaluates the model performance and outputs the settings which achieved the best results. As the algorithm is based on a brute-force, it is computationally expensive [34].

Random Search: The algorithm, rather than trying each parameter configuration (as grid search), randomly selects the parameters, evaluates them and selects the best configuration based on a given metric. Random search is able to find models which are just as good or even better than grid search but in a fraction of its computational time [5].

Bayesian optimization: In contrast to random and grid search, Bayesian optimization keeps track of previous optimization results and any prior information in order to help the exploration of the search space. The algorithm is based on the Bayes' theorem and aims to optimize an objective function that selects the hyper-parameters. Bayesian optimization has shown that it is able to find superior results to human experts or state-of-the-art approaches [49]

Tree-structured Parzen Estimator Approach (TPE): Similarly to the Bayesian optimization TPE also constructs probabilistic models based on previous evaluations in order to approximate the performance of hyper-parameters. The algorithm uses Parzen Estimators to create densities where samples are taken and evaluated [6].

Hyper-parameter optimization is a costly procedure requiring lots of computational resources. Another question arising from hyper-parameter optimization is not only how to select the parameters but how to allocate the resources for the randomly selected hyper-parameter configurations. Li et al. [33] developed a novel algorithm called Hyperband which early stops poorly performing configurations. Hyperband uses a method called Successive Halving (SHA) which for a given amount of resources evaluates all configurations, keeps the best ones and repeats the same step until only one configuration remains. Moreover, Hyperband eliminates incorrectly early stopping configurations by evaluating the configurations on a different number of resources. Other approaches use similar methods. Asynchronous SHA (ASHA) [32] also uses SHA but effectively paralyses early stooping and configuration promotion, making it suitable for large-scale hyper-parameter optimization problems.

3.2.6 Transfer Learning

The classical paradigm for supervised machine learning is to train a model based on a single dataset. This requires a large amount of data which is often not available. Moreover, for each task and problem, a new model is trained from scratch [47] which is time and resource consuming. Transfer learning aims to solve these problems and reduce over-fitting and to improve performance by transferring or adapting knowledge from one problem or dataset to another [39]. By sharing pre-trained models between different problems, the models also generalize better. Indeed, one of the most promising advances in NLP applications also came from transfer learning [47].

Pretrained models can be used in two ways for a given problem [47]:

1. Feature Extraction: The pretrained model is used as a feature extractor where the features are used as inputs for a separate model. In this case the weights of the pretrained model are frozen.

2. Fine-tuning: This approach consists of two steps. First, the pretrained model is frozen and only the model is trained. Next, the weights of the pretrained model are unfrozen and the entire network is trained together.

A common form of transfer learning in NLP applications is to use pre-trained word embeddings. Word embedding is the representation of words as real-valued vectors by encoding their meaning, such that words with similar meanings are closer in the vector space than dissimilar ones. One of the most widely used word embeddings are GloVE, ELMO or Word2Vec.

3.2.7 BERT

Bidirectional Encoder Representations from Transformers (BERT) is a language representation model which trains Transformer encoders [20] bidirectionally. As opposed to LSTMs which learn the input sequence left-to-right or right-to-left, Transformer encoders read the input sequence at once. The training of BERT consists of two steps. First some input tokens are masked and the model has to predict the original tokens. This is called masked LM (MLM). Then, in order for the model to learn relationships between two sentences, the model is trained to predict the next sentence from a corpus. This is called next sentence prediction (NSP). Results from BERT show that it achieves new state-of-the-art results in a variety of NLP tasks such as MultiNLI, SQuAD and pushes the GLUE score by 7.7% [20].

3.3 Conclusion

Several design choices have to be made for bot detectors which require the theoretical background introduced above. In addition, there are many solutions to the given problem, which means the design space is large. In the following lines the theoretical design choices such as why certain algorithms or ANN architectures are used instead of others will be discussed.

The biggest question is which neural network model to use as the base model of the detector. As described earlier, ANNs are not suitable for NLP problems; therefore, LSTMs will be used. Regarding hyper-parameter optimization, TPE will be applied using ASHA, as they have shown promising results. As for transfer learning, feature extraction will be used for word embeddings; fine-tuning will be used for constructing a BERT based bot detector; and for data augmentation, a new approach will be introduced in the next chapter.

CHAPTER 4

Implementation

4.1 Data Understanding

The dataset of the PAN 2019 Bots and Gender Profiling task is split into three sets, namely training (2800 accounts), validation (1240 accounts) and test (2640 accounts) sets. Each account has 100 tweets and an account can belong to a human or a bot. In this section, the data exploration of the training set will be discussed and explained.

In order to avoid bias for supervised machine learning algorithms the dataset has to be balanced. The training dataset contains 1400 humans and 1400 bots making it ideal for machine learning algorithms (see Figure 4.1).

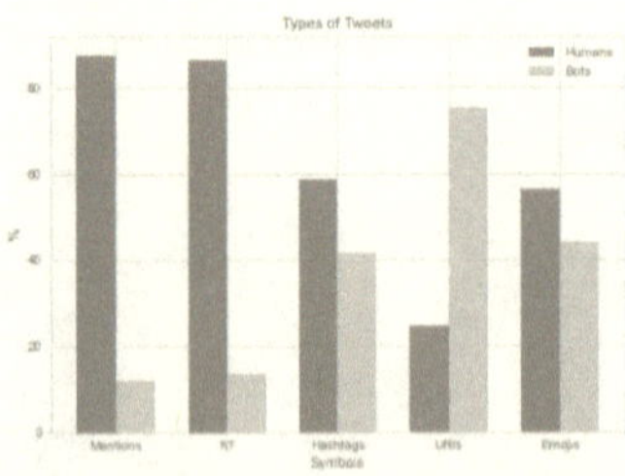

Figure 4.1: Symbol usage

Figure 4.2 shows the most frequent tokens for the entire corpus which also include stopwords (such as 'the', 'to' or 'and') or URLs (https). These tokens will have to be preprocessed during the data preparation phase of the implementation in order to reduce the dimensionality of the corpus. It is also interesting to see how the most frequent tokens differ between humans and bots. As can be seen on Figure 4.3 humans and bots both share links (co, https, https) but bots use these tokens at a higher rate. Moreover, bots share content containing tokens such as hiring, developer, engineer and software which can be an indication of job promotion and spamming behaviour.

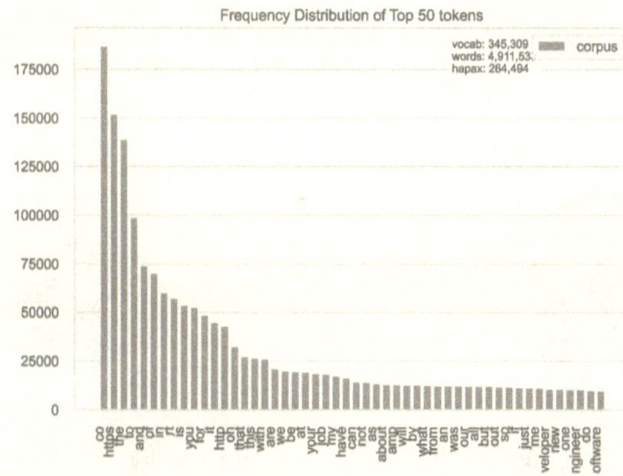

Figure 4.2: Most Frequently used tokens by Bots and Humans.

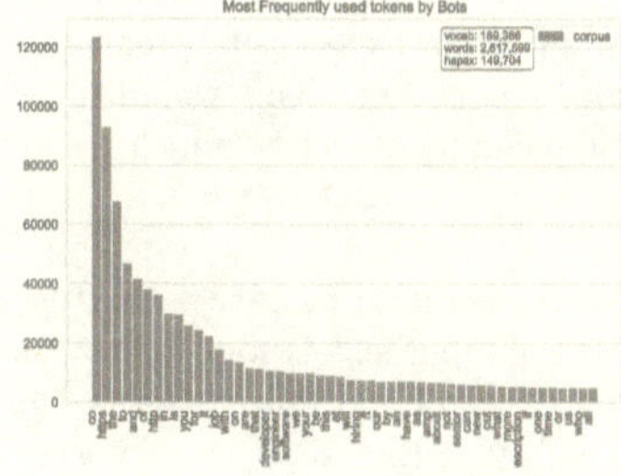

(a) Most Frequently used tokens: Bots.

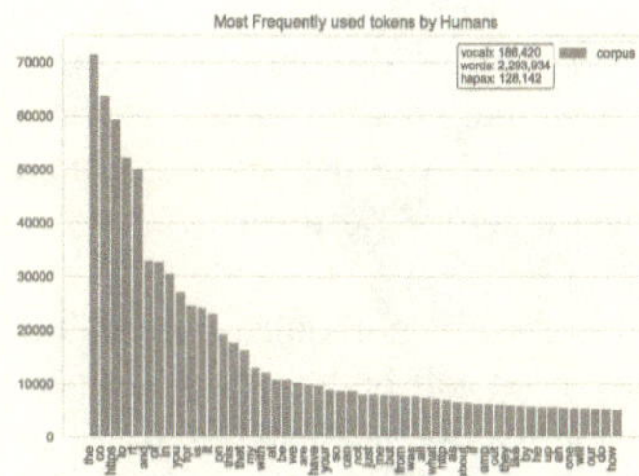

(b) Most Frequently used tokens: Humans.

Figure 4.3: Most frequent tokens

As the predictive models are built on word embeddings, an important aspect is the sequence length of the tweets. Figure 4.4 demonstrates the distribution of the number of tokens within a tweet. Most tweets have less than 25 tokens, but some have more than 40, and one has almost 100 words. It is also worth looking into which type of account (bots or humans) prefer using which type of Twitter key words such as hashtags, mentions, emojis or URLs. Based on Figure 4.1, humans retweet and use hashtags and mentions more than bots. On the other hand, bots post more than three times as many URLs as humans, indicating malicious activity.

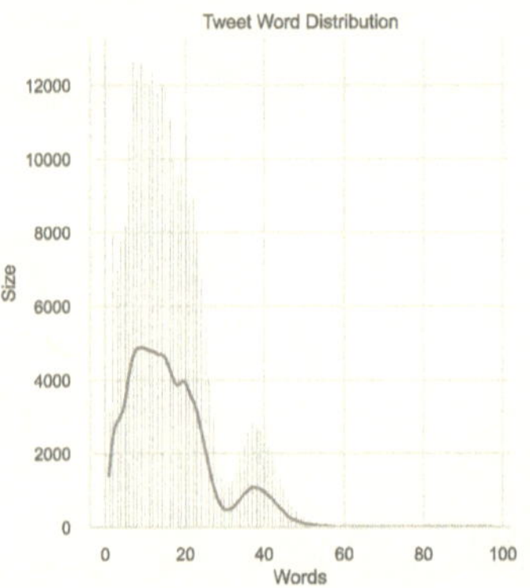

Figure 4.4: Tweet length distribution.

4.2 Data Preparation

The bot detectors which will be introduced shortly use GloVE as a pre-trained word embedding. During the data preparation phase an important aspect is to preprocess the data in a similar manner as the authors of the word embedding. This would allow the predictive model to learn the semantic and syntatic meaning of words, which could also boost the detectors' performance.

As word embeddings require a fixed input size, tweets also need to have a fixed length. There is a trade-off between the sequence length. If the input size is too small, valuable information may be neglected and the models may not learn important patterns. On the other hand, if the input is too large, the dimensionality of the corpus may permit the predictive models to learn. There are many common strategies for handling this, nevertheless, in this work, based on Figure 4.4, the maximum tweet length will be limited to Q3 + 1.5*IQR 40 tokens/tweet. This means that tweets which have more than 40 tokens will be truncated and tweets with a smaller size will be padded.

The data set was preprocessed as follows:

1. HTML tags were removed.

2. URLs were replaced with a <url>tag.

3. Mentions were replaced with a <user>tag.

4. Hashtags were replaced with a <hashtag>tag. Moreover, word segmentation was applied in order to split hashtags into their corresponding word(s). For example, #HashTag is represented as <hashtag>hash tag.

5. Numbers were replaced with a <number>tag.

6. Emojis were mapped to a tag, such as <smile>, <sadface><heart>etc.

7. Accented characters were removed.

8. Repeated characters were replaced with an <elong>tag. For example ... is represented as . <elong>.

9. Contractions were fixed.

10. Upper case tokens were replaced with <allcaps>and were lower cased.

11. Special characters such as ", !, ? etc. were surrounded by spaces.

12. Tweets were lower cased and extra spaces were removed.

Additional preprocessing steps had also been experimented such as using named entity recognition to replace words based on their entity, removing punctuations, stop words and lemmatizing the corpus. Unfortunately, these steps did not improve the accuracy; hence, they were omitted from the data preprocessing steps.

4.3   Modeling Approaches

This section introduces different modeling approaches, which were implemented during the modeling phase. 12 deep-learning-based methods will be discussed here, which will be evaluated in the Evaluation chapter of the **book**. The core of seven models are based on LSTM networks, four are based on BERT models and one a combination of the two. The detectors were written in Python and the deep-learning models are built using Pytorch.

4.3.1 Tweet Classification

All models introduced in this chapter build on a predictor which can classify individual tweets as humans or bots. The aim of this model is to classify tweets and based on the individual predictions new models can be trained which can classify the accounts. From here on, this model will be referenced as Tweet Classifier.

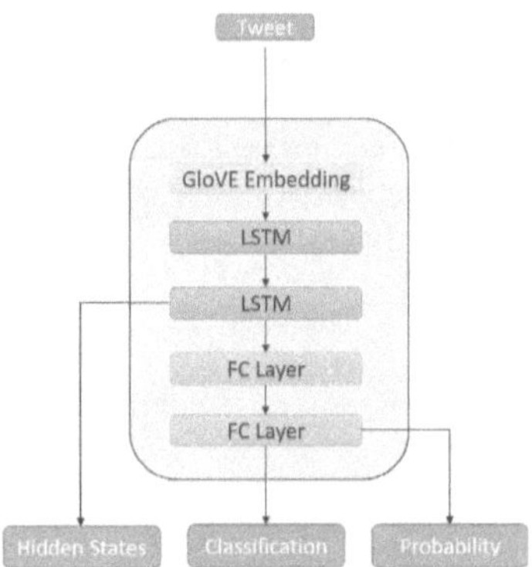

Figure 4.5: Tweet Classifier

Figure 4.5 shows the architecture of the Tweet Classifier. After preprocessing the data, the sequences of the token indexes are fed into the GloVE embedding, which creates the embedding representation of the tokens. Next, a two-layer bidirectional LSTM model learns the patterns of the tweets and finally, two fully connected layers output the prediction. The model outputs the classification, the probability of a tweet being bot and the hidden states of the last LSTM layer. These outputs will be used by models which classify the individual accounts.

Figure 4.6 gives an example of a prediction. The tweet is first preprocessed as described in the data preparation phase, next the tokens are converted to padded indexes and finally the Tweet Classifier makes the prediction.

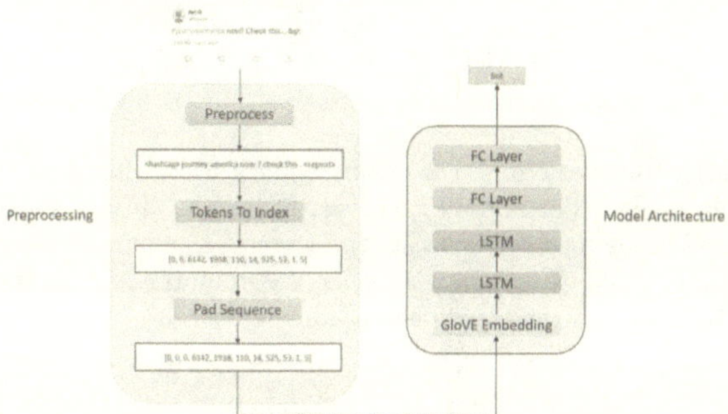

Figure 4.6: An example of a prediction

4.3.2 Majority Vote

In order to classify an account one could simply feed the individual tweets to the Tweet Classifier, collect the predictions and, based on a majority vote, classify the account. Figure 4.7 demonstrates the architecture of a bot detector using a majority vote. This approach does not require the implementation of additional models, which makes it fast to train and use.

4.3.3 Probability Based Prediction

A similar approach to the majority vote is to use tweet probabilities rather than classification predictions. In this scenario, the account's probability is calculated by averaging the sum of each of its tweets' probability. If the account probability is larger than 0.5, the account is considered a bot, otherwise a human. The advantage of this method over the majority based prediction is that certainty of the Twee Classifier is also taken in to

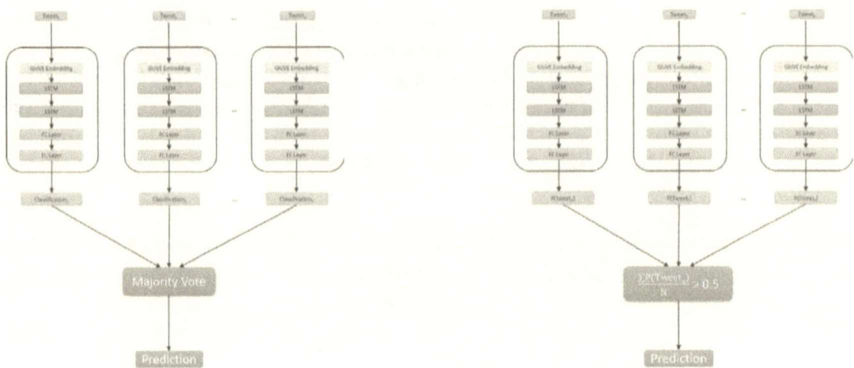

Figure 4.7: Majority Vote (left) and Probability based prediction (right).

consideration during the prediction. For example given 51 tweets of an account have a probability of 0.49 being a bot and 49 tweets with a probability of 1 being a bot, the majority vote based predictor would classify the account as a human, whereas the probability based account would classify it as a bot, as based on the probabilities the account has a higher likely-hood of being a bot than a human.

4.3.4 Combined Model

The output of the Tweet Classifier can also be the input of an account classifier model. For this approach, each tweet of an account is first fed into the Tweet Classifier model and the hidden representation of the tweet is used as inputs for a second model to classify accounts. The individual hidden states are first collected, then used as inputs for the second model.

In this model configuration, the Tweet classifier learns the features and most important characteristics of tweets regarding their originality. The hidden states represent this information; therefore the Tweet Classifier serves as an encoder where the model's output is disregarded.

The model consists of two LSTM layers and a fully connected layer which outputs the prediction for a given account (see Figure 4.8). Moreover, during the implementation, 5-fold cross validation was used, where 5 independent models were trained on different partitions of the training set. The prediction of the models is based on the majority vote of the 5 predictions or based on the average of the 5 probabilities, creating an ensembled configuration.

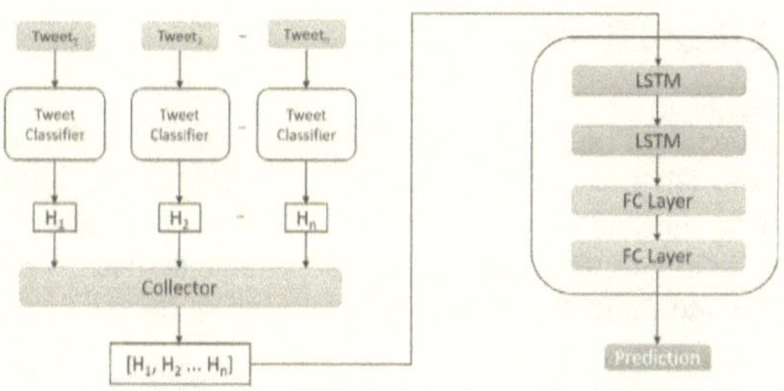

Figure 4.8: An example of a prediction

4.3.5 Fine-tuning BERT

BERT has also been fine-tuned to classify tweets as bots or humans. For this task, the pre-trained BertForSequenceClassification model was used from the hugging face library. The preprocessing steps described earlier are irrelevant for BERT as BERT requires special preprocessing. First, the input sequence was tokenized, all sentences were padded or truncated to a constant length, and special tags were added to the beginning and ending of each input [CLS]/[SEP]. Embeddings are also not required for BERT models as the pre-trained model already has one.

Regarding the account classification, the same steps had been tried as described for the LSTM models that is, majority vote, probability-based account prediction and representing each tweet as the last hidden state of BERT and feeding them to the same combined LSTM model. Figure 4.9 demonstrates the architecture of how a fine-tuned BERT model combined with an LSTM model can classify accounts. Moreover, the LSTM based account classifier was also trained on the hidden states of a BERT model wich was not fine-tuned.

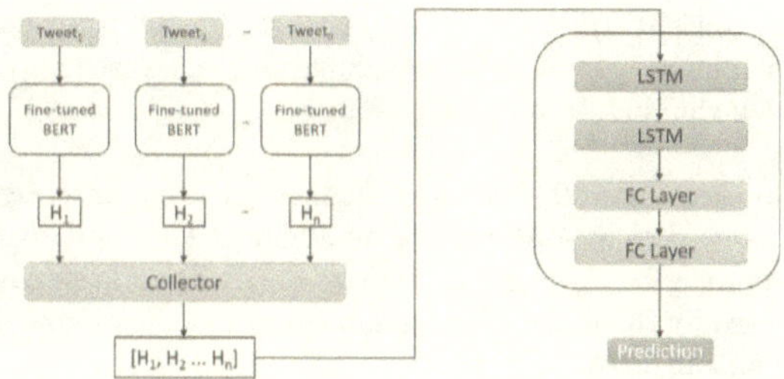

Figure 4.9: Fine-tuned BERT combined with an account classifier LSTM Model

4.3.6   Combining Hidden States

The hidden states of BERT and the LSTM Tweet Classifier can also be combined. As can be seen on Figure 4.10 the information of the BERT model, hidden size of 768 and the LSTM Tweet classifier, hidden size of 32 are concatenated and are fed into the LSTM Account Classifier. This approach allows the account classifier to learn from both the BERT and LSTM models which may supplement each other.

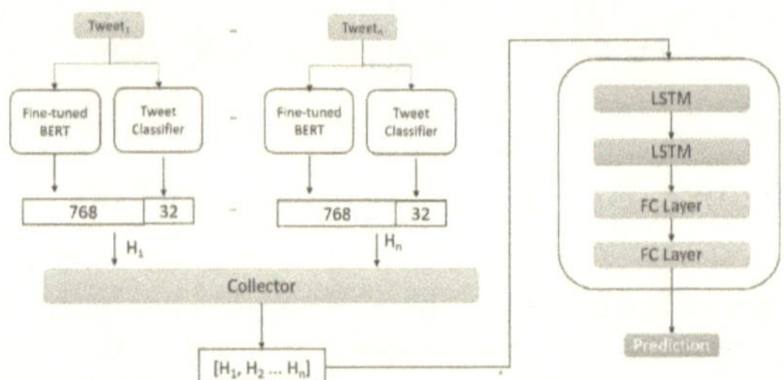

Figure 4.10: Hidden State Concatenation

4.4   Data Augmentation

As the training set has less than 3k accounts, training the LSTM based account classifier network is quite challenging. In order to overcome this issue data augmentation was used on the hidden states of the accounts. Let A be the set of $\{T1, T2...T_n\}$ representing an account with n tweets and the set of the hidden states H=$\{H1, H2...H_n\}$. We define an augmentation function f(H, l) where $l \leq n$, which returns all n-l consecutive subsets of H of length l. This augmentation method significantly increased the availability of the training data, which should also increase the accuracy of the model.

In addition to the above, tweets were also augmented using an external library called nlpaug[1], which was used as a word embedding augmenter. The data augmentation was applied on the preprocessed data, as on the raw data URLs, hashtags and emojis were incorrectly segmented by the library. The augmenter used GloVE and substituted tokens based on embedding similarity.

4.5   Hyper-parameter Selection

This section discusses model configuration selection along with hyper-parameter optimization.

Ray-Tune [35] was used for hyper-parameter optimization using TPE as the search algorithm and ASHA to early terminate bad configurations. From here on, a training run with a fixed hyper-parameter configuration will be referred to as a trial.

4.5.1   Tweet Classifier

In order to find the best configuration 30 trials were executed running for a maximum of 20 epochs using Stochastic Gradient Descent (SGD) as the optimization algorithm and Binary Cross Entropy (BCE) as the loss function. The following hyper-parameter search space was used:

- Learning rate: 0.0001-0.2

- LSTM hidden size: 32, 64, 128, 356

- LSTM layers: 1,2

- Batch size: 32, 64

- Fully Connected Layer size: 32, 64, 128, 256

- LSTM dropout: 0.0-0.5

- Fully Connected Layer dropout: 0.0-0.5

- weight decay: 0-0.1

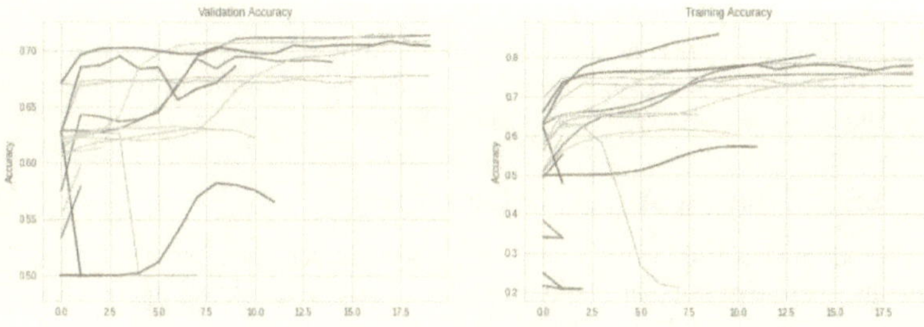

Figure 4.11: Training and Validation Accuracy of Trials

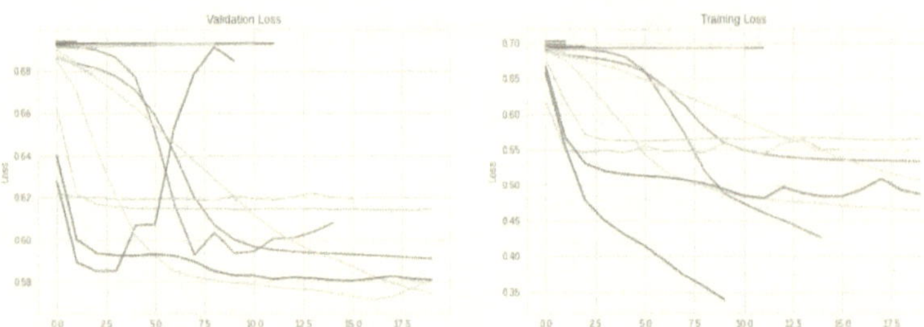

Figure 4.12: Training and Validation Loss of Trials

As can be seen in Figures 4.11 and 4.12, several bad trials early terminated, whereas the promising trials finished the 20 epochs. As the trials only ran for 20 epochs after the parameter optimization the best configuration was found manually by increasing the epochs for the most promising configurations.

4.5.2 BERT

The authors of BERT [20] recommend choosing the hyper-parameters from a pre-defined set of configurations. Therefore, exploring the search space can be done with a couple of iterations. For the tweet classification problem, the following parameters achieved the highest validation accuracy:

- Learning rate: 2e-5

- Batch size: 32

- epsilon: 1e-8

- max sequence length: 100

- epochs: 4

The sequence length was determined by the distribution of the number of tokens within the tweets after preprocessing since BERT also generates sub words of the tokens, which increases the dimensionality of the input data.

4.5.3 LSTM based Account Classifier

Three different models had been constructed for account classification, one for the BERT based hidden representation, one for the Tweet Classifier based tweet representation and one which combines the hidden states of BERT and the Tweet classifier. Moreover, different models had been evaluated using the original data and the augmented data. It is also important to highlight that an additional preprocessing step lies before the execution of the account classifier which serves to normalize the hidden states of the tweets.

Model	LR	Hidden Size	Layers	Batch Size	FC Size	LSTM Droput	FC Droput	L2
Tweet Classifier	0.00100	32	1	64	128	0.400	0.100	0.1
BERT	0.00100	768	-	64	-	-	-	-

Table 4.1: Best hyper-parameters for tweet classification.

Model	LR	Hidden Size	Layers	Batch Size	FC Size	LSTM Droput	FC Droput	L2
Account Classfier (LSTM, LSTM)	0.00800	32	2	64	128	0.499	0.900	9.1e-08
Account Classifier + Aug. (LSTM, LSTM)	0.00890	64	2	64	32	0.466	0.055	1.1e-06
Account Classifier (BERT, LSTM)	0.00040	128	2	64	512	0.088	0.100	6.7e-06
Account Classifier + Aug. (BERT, LSTM)	0.00329	512	2	64	32	0.198	0.500	2.8e-06
Account Classifier (BERT w/o fine-tuning, LSTM)	0.00017	256	1	32	32	0.402	0.176	3.9e-07
Account Classifier (BERT + LSTM, LSTM)	0.00171	128	2	64	64	0.4661	0.1055	9.9e-06

Table 4.2: Best hyper-parameters for account classification.

In order to find the best configurations for each model configuration, hyper-parameter optimization was used. 30 trials were executed and evaluated against the validation set for a maximum of 100 epochs. TPE and ASHA were used for exploring the search space and for early terminating bad trials. Table 4.1 and 4.2 shows the hyper-parameters of each model.

4.6 Software Architecture

Figure 4.13 demonstrates the software architecture of the **book** work. During the design phase, the main objective was to create classes that have only one responsibility and can be easily extended with new functionalities. Below is a summary of each class:

- DataUnderstander: Class used for data exploration and which creates several plots such as distributions of tweets or tokens, boxplots and bar charts of the input data.

- Preprocessor: Responsible for preprocessing the raw data as specified by the data preparation phase earlier.

- DataSetLoader: Reads the XML files and constructs the accounts, tweets and target labels for the training validation and test sets.

- Optimizer: Responsible for the hyper-parameter optimization of the models.

- Evaluator: Evaluates the models on the test set and creates metrics.

- Model: Abstract class for all modeling classes, holds the methods which all models have to implement.

- TweetClassifier: Implements the Tweet Classifier model, which was described in chapter 4.3.1.

- AccountClassifier: Implements the Account Classifier model which was described in chapter 4.3.4.

- BertDetector: Contains the fine-tuned BERT model which was previously described in more detail in chapter 4.3.5.

- TweetAugmenter: Generates new tweets as described in chapter 4.4.

- DataAugmenter: Augments the hidden states of the tweet classifier or of the hidden sequence representations from the fine-tuned BERT model.

- DatasetMaper: Overrides torch.utils.data.Dataset holds the input data and target attributes which is used by TweetClassifier.

- DatasetMaperList: Overrides torch.utils.data.Dataset holds the input data, sequence length and target attributes for the AccountClassifier.

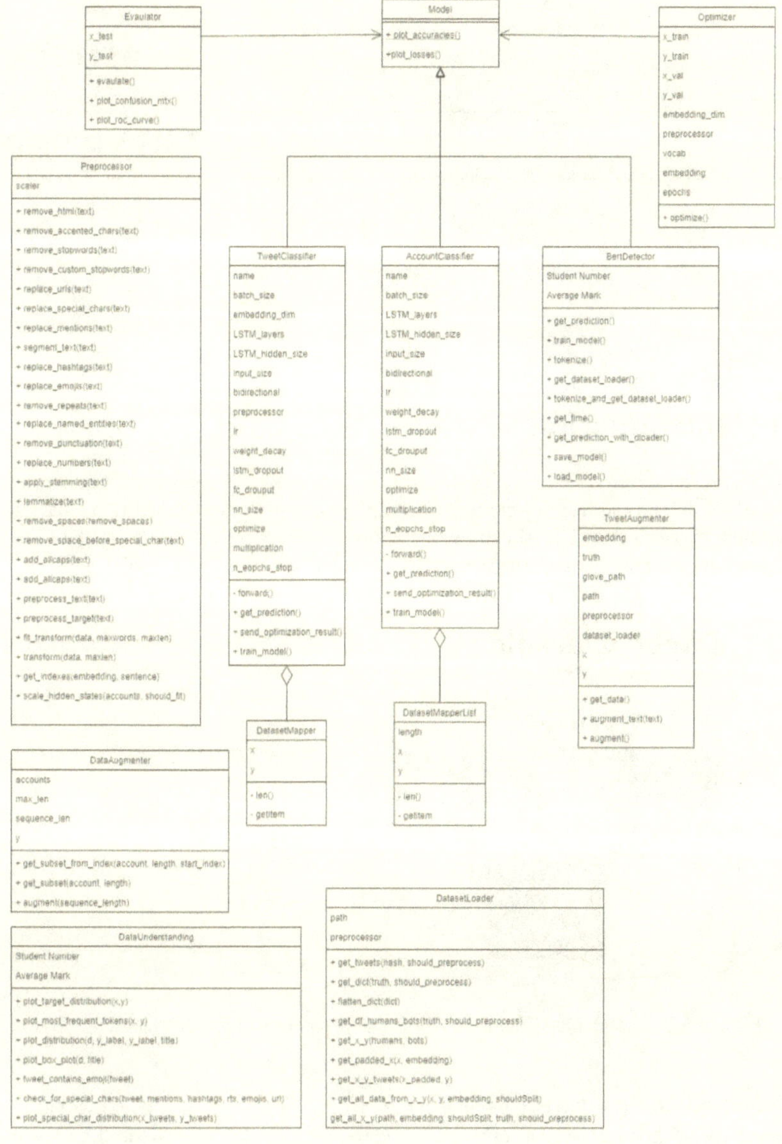

Figure 4.13: Class Diagram

CHAPTER 5

Evaluation

5.1 Introduction

This chapter evaluates and analyses the proposed models from chapter 4. The test set will be used while the models are configured employing the highest performing parameters described in more detail in the previous chapter. Four novel metrics will be used to evaluate the models, namely the accuracy, F1 score, precision and recall.

5.2 Tweet Classifier

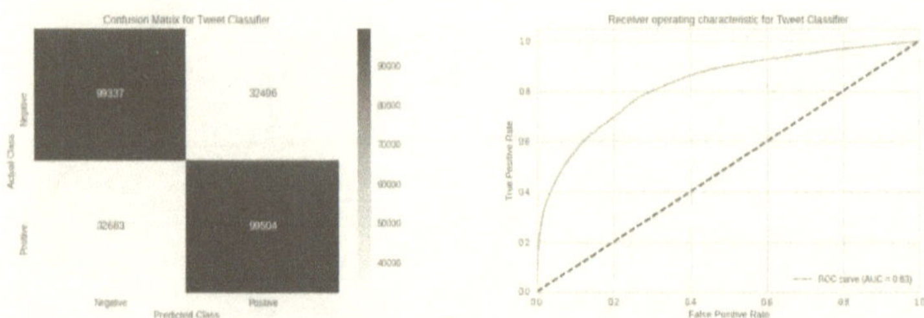

Figure 5.1: Tweet Classification - Left: Confusion Matrix. Right: ROC Curve

In this section, the Tweet Classifier model will be evaluated on the individual tweets. Moreover, the account predictability of the classifier will also be evaluated by the earlier mentioned majority vote and probability-based prediction.

The Tweet Classifier model reached an accuracy, f1 score, precision and recall of 0.75. This means the model is not biased towards any of the classes. Figure 5.1 shows the confusion matrix and the ROC curve where the AUC is 0.83.

Predicting accounts using majority vote achieves an accuracy of 0.87 and 0.86 for the F1 score. On the other hand, the probability-based account prediction reaches 0.879 accuracy and 0.87 F1 score beating the majority vote by 0.8%.

5.3 Fine-tuned BERT Model

The fine-tuned BERT model classifies individual tweets with an accuracy of 0.82, F1 score of 0.80 and AUC score of 0.91. In Figure 5.2, we can see the ROC curve and the confusion matrix. We can clearly see the model predicts almost 40k accounts as bots where as they were actually humans.

When predicting the accounts with a majority vote, the fine-tuned BERT model had an accuracy and F1 score of 0.849 while the probability-based prediction yielded an accuracy of 0.851 and 0.83 F1 score. This is almost 3% less than the LSTM based account prediction, while the BERT model predicts tweets 7% better.

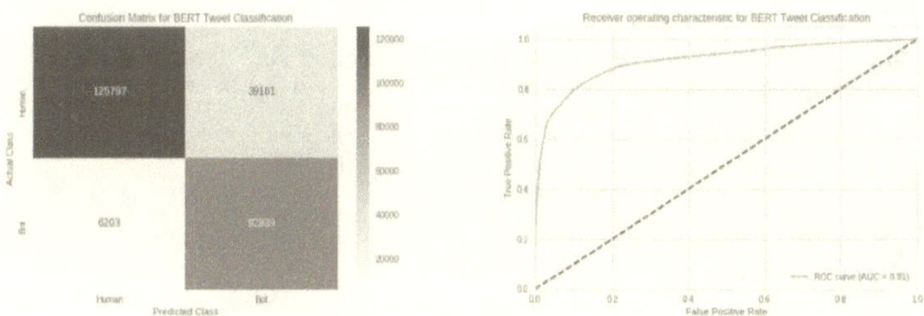

Figure 5.2: BERT Tweet Classification - Left: Confusion Matrix. Right: ROC Curve

5.4 Combined Model using Tweet Classifier

This section focuses on the combined LSTM models, namely with and without data augmentation. Furthermore, as described in the previous chapter, the results presented here are an average of 5 different models.

The model without data augmentation on average yielded an accuracy of 0.89 and F1

score of 0.89. On the other hand, with data augmentation, the model only reached an
accuracy of 0.88 and F1 score of 0.881, which is 1% less than the model trained on the
data that was not augmented.

5.5 Combined Model using BERT

Although the fine-tuned BERT model reached the highest accuracy for predicting individual tweets, the combined model using the hidden states from BERT did not achieve
superior results.

Without data augmentation, the combined model reached an accuracy of 0.836 and an F1
score of 0.828. Similarly to the Tweet Classifier based combined approach, without data
augmentation the model performed slightly better than with data augmentation. The
model yielded an accuracy of 0.835 and F1 score of 0.821. Although the model without
data augmentation performed slightly better, augmentation did not make a recognizable
difference. It is also important to mention, the combined model with the BERT model
which was not fine-tuned yielded an accuracy of 0.806 which is almost 3% less than if
the fine-tuned BERT model was used.

5.6 Combining Hidden States

After combining the hidden states of both the fine-tuned BERT and LSTM models, the
model yielded an accuracy of 0.838 and an F1 score of 0.82 on the test set. Although,
the account classifier could use the information of both models it wasn't able to predict
accounts better than the Account classifier based on BERT.

5.7 Summary of the results

Table 5.1, 5.2 and 5.3 demonstrates the results of all 13 models designed in this work. As
can be seen the combined LSTM model yielded the highest accuracy of 0.892. Although
the fine-tuned BERT model classifies individual tweets at the highest rate (0.828), all
LSTM based models performed better during the account classification, including models
based on majority vote and probability-based predictions.

The results are somewhat surprising as one would expect current state-of-the-art BERT

Model	Accuracy	F1	Precision	Recall
LSTM Tweet Classifier	0.753	0.753	0.753	0.754
BERT Tweet Classifier	**0.828**	**0.800**	**0.937**	**0.700**

Table 5.1: Tweet classification results.

Model	Accuracy	F1	Precision	Recall
Tweet Classifier - Majority Vote	0.873	0.864	0.930	0.806
Tweet Classifier - Probability based pred.	**0.878**	**0.870**	**0.936**	**0.811**
BERT - Majority Vote	0.849	0.826	0.975	0.717
BERT - Probability based pred.	0.852	0.830	0.976	0.721

Table 5.2: Account classification results based on single models.

Model	Accuracy	F1	Precision	Recall
Account Classifier - Majority Vote (LSTM, LSTM)	0.891	0.890	0.895	0.886
Account Classifier - Probability based pred. (LSTM, LSTM)	**0.892**	**0.893**	**0.881**	**0.906**
Account Classifier + Augmentation (LSTM, LSTM)	0.880	0.880	0.878	0.884
Account Classifier - Majority Vote (BERT, LSTM)	0.836	0.828	0.872	0.787
Account Classifier - Probability based pred. (BERT, LSTM)	0.838	0.830	0.874	0.790
Account Classifier + Augmentation (BERT, LSTM)	0.835	0.821	0.903	0.753
Account Classifier (BERT w/o Fine-tuning, LSTM)	0.806	0.793	0.853	0.740
Account Classifier (BERT + LSTM, LSTM)	0.838	0.820	0.916	0.743

Table 5.3: Account classification results based on multiple models.

based models to be superior to LSTM based approaches. In the next chapter, the results
will be discussed, including the challenges faced during the implementation. Moreover, an
explanation will be given of the under-performance of the BERT and data augmentation
based models.

CHAPTER 6

Discussion

This chapter summarizes and discusses how the PAN 2019 Bots and Gender Profiling task was solved and how the results compare to the baseline models summarized in chapter 2. Furthermore, this chapter will also reflect on the research questions formalized in Chapter 1.

6.1 Discussion of the results

In order to solve the bot detection task of the PAN 2019 Bots and Gender Profiling task, 13 different deep-learning based models were designed, implemented and evaluated. Some models are basic in the sense that they can only classify individual tweets; others are more complex and combine different deep-learning models such as LSTMs with fine-tuned Transformer encoders to classify accounts as bots or humans.

The best result was achieved by combining two LSTM models, one to classify individual tweets as humans or bots, and another which takes the hidden states from the first model and classifies the inspected account. This approach yielded an accuracy of 0.89. Surprisingly, augmenting the input data for this model resulted in a 1% decrease in the accuracy. Although, data augmentation typically increases the accuracy of machine learning models, there can be several reasons why the model did not perform better. One reason is that during the hyper-parameter optimization, the search space was ill-defined and the optimization algorithm did not explore configurations that reach a high performance. On the other hand, maybe the augmented data was too complex and the model could not learn all the patterns. This can explain why the training accuracy was not improving while the validation accuracy was during training.

Another interesting point is that although the fine-tuned BERT model predicts the individual tweets better (+6%) than the LSTM based tweet classifier, the majority and probability-based account predictions are worse than the majority or probability predictions of the LSTM tweet classifier. This can be because of two factors. First, the

BERT model has a low recall which means many human accounts are classified as bots; second, the distribution of the incorrect tweets are spanned across more accounts than the LSTM based classifier, which can have a significant impact during the account classification. Moreover, the LSTM account classifier model performed poorer with the BERT hidden states. Again, this could be because of the incorrect hyper parameter configurations of the LSTM account classifier, or the hidden representation of the tweets are too similar; that is, the LSTM model cannot differentiate humans and bots.

It is also important to highlight that the LSTM based tweet classifier classifies accounts just 1% lower than the highest performing model introduced in this work. However, it can be trained in a fraction of the training time of a complex model such as fine-tuning BERT or the combined LSTM models.

6.2 Comparison of the best results of the PAN 2019 Author Profiling task

The best results and the majority of the PAN 2019 Bots and Gender Profiling task sumbmissions solved the task by classical machine learning algorithms (see Chapter 2 for more information). The top 3 submissions achieved more than 0.94 accuracy and these results serve as a benchmark for this work. The work presented here is based on deep-learning methods; moreover, only the textual data was used to train the models without additional metadata. On the other hand, the benchmarked solutions all extracted features from the data; therefore, it is hard to compare them. In summary it can be stated that the work presented is not superior to the benchmarked solutions and further improvements should be made to improve performance.

6.3 Reflection on the research questions

The book work aims at answering three research questions, which are described in Chapter 1. Referring to RQ1 of Chapter 1, whether deep-learning based approaches can compete with classical machine learning algorithms on the limited dataset: it can be argued that deep-learning based methods, especially LSTM based models, achieved good but not superior results.

For RQ2 in Chapter 1, data augmentation did not improve the accuracy because of the already mentioned reasons, such as by incorrectly specifying the hyper-parameter search space or incorrect implementation. Nevertheless, data augmentation in the NLP domain is challenging and an area that needs to be researched.

Regarding RQ3 of Chapter 1, it is clear that pre-trained models and language representations do improve the results. The fine-tuned BERT model beat the LSTM based tweet classification model by almost 7%.

Chapter 7

Conclusion and Future Work

7.1 Summary

The present **book** work gives the reader an overview of the area of automatized social media bots and, their detection methods. The work can be broken down into a theoretical and a practical part.

During the literature review, an overview is presented of the evolution of bots, their detectors and current state-of-the-art bot detection approaches, including several examples of supervised, unsupervised and adversarial methods. Challenges are also described, such as the difficulties of data collection. Chapter 3 focuses on the fundamentals of this work. The theoretical background of the proposed bot detection approaches is introduced, such as how RNNs work, how hyper-parameters can be optimized or how transfer learning can be used.

Chapter 4 and 5 focus on the design, implementation and evaluation of 13 deep-learning based detectors. A data augmentation approach is implemented and described for this task. The selection of the hyper-parameters is also discussed. Finally, in Chapter 6, the results are discussed and the research questions are answered.

7.2 Conclusion

The bot detectors introduced here successfully solve bot detection with an accuracy reaching almost 0.90. Although it can be argued, the presented deep-learning models are not superior to traditional classical machine learning methods. Having said that, the data set was quite limited in size and on large scale data the outcome may have been different. In addition, to the best of my knowledge, the presented architecture of the combining LSTM/BERT models with another LSTM model for classifying accounts have not been researched before. Therefore, this work can also serve as a baseline for future improvements for deep-learning based approaches.

7.3   Further development

Even though the work presented here solves the task, there are several improvements to be explored. In the following paragraphs, two future improvements will be described, namely, how data augmentation methods could be used to improve the data set and what other deep-learning architectures could be applied to improve the performance of the models.

7.3.1   Data Augmentation

In Chapter 4, it was mentioned that text augmentation was also experimented by randomly substituting tokens based on embedding similarity using GloVE. Although, at the time, it did not improve accuracy, due to time constraints this approach was not fully explored. In the future, text augmentation will be applied, such as the approach by Wei et al. [58], which combines synonym replacement, random insertion, random swap and random deletion.

7.3.2 Different Deep-learning approaches

One of the challenges faced during the **book** work was that the complex models did not improve the accuracy as much as it was expected. The reasons were described in the previous chapter and the improvements will be described in the next lines.

One way to improve the models is by making architectural changes to them, such as by adding more fully connected layers, using different loss functions or optimizers. One could also replace LSTMs by GRUs or use different word embeddings which all may improve the overall accuracy.

Another approach could be to improve the hidden representation of the models by using Siamese neural networks [13]. These networks are trained to predict whether two input samples are the same or not by calculating the similarity of the inputs (for example, images of two people). These networks have shown great results in computer vision in the area of face verification, but they could also be used to improve the bot detection models of this work. If a Siamese network were to be used, which is trained on tweets of humans and bots, the model would be forced to learn the characteristics of bots and humans in order to differentiate them. Therefore, the hidden representations of the tweets would also be more similar if they came from the same account or same type of accounts such as a bot or a human. These hidden states could then be used by the account classification model, which was introduced earlier.

And last, the best models from the PAN 2019 Bots and Gender Profiling task could also be combined with the approaches introduced in this **book** work as the solutions could be complementary to each other.